Play in The Faith

Vol. 2

Conduct & Behavior

ISBN: 978-1674105321

Michael Ray Garvin

<u>DEDICATION</u>

Heavenly Father, I thank You for your mercy and grace. I pray that this book helps believers in Jesus, live a life that is pleasing to You!

CONTENTS

Scripture   i

1) Words Of Heaven…………………..   1

2) Swear Not At All…………………….   9

3) Live Holy & Play Holy………………   17

4) Be Truthful In All Things…………….   22

5) Freedom From Vanity………………   27

6) Don't Be Anxious……………………   37

7) The Forgiven Must Forgive…………   42

SCRIPTURE

13 So brace up your minds; *be sober* (circumspect, morally alert); set your hope wholly and unchangeably on the grace (divine favor) that is coming to you when Jesus Christ (the Messiah) is revealed.

14 [Live] as **children of obedience** [to God]; **do not conform yourselves to the evil desires** [that governed you] in your former ignorance [when you did not know the requirements of the Gospel].

15 But as the One Who called you is holy, **you yourselves also be holy in all your conduct and manner of living**.

16 For it is written, You shall be holy, for I am holy.

1 Peter 1:13-16 AMPC

CHAPTER 1

WORDS OF HEAVEN

Praise the Lord for He is good! I am truly thankful to have a relationship with Jesus. He has been so merciful to me and my family. I strive every day to live a life that is pleasing to Him. Let's look at how we can please our Lord Jesus, with our words.

> •[18] For there **are many**, of whom I have often told you and now tell you even with tears, who walk (live) as enemies of the cross of Christ (the Anointed One).
> [19] They are doomed *and* their fate is eternal misery (perdition); **their god is their stomach (their appetites, their sensuality)** and they

glory in their shame, _siding with earthly_
things and being of their party.
20 But **we are citizens** of the state
(commonwealth, homeland) which is **in**
heaven, and from it also
we earnestly _and_ patiently await [the coming
of] the Lord Jesus Christ (the Messiah) [as]
Savior,
Philippians 3:20 AMPC

The Apostle Paul is saying that we are
citizens of Heaven. In verses 18-19 of Philippians 3,
he talks about people who mind earthly things and
their end is destruction.

The word mind in the Greek is **phroneō**- _(to_
have understanding, to be wise, to seek, to feel, to
think, to strive for).

These people are more concerned about
earthly things than heavenly things. As believers in
Jesus, our citizenship is in heaven, and our speech
should be words of Heaven.

⇒As followers of Jesus, our words are very important. Jesus said that our words will either **JUSTIFY** or **CONDEMN** us.

36 But I say unto you, That ***every idle word*** that men shall speak, they shall give account thereof in the day of judgment.
37 For **by thy words** thou shalt be ***justified***, and **by thy words** thou shalt be ***condemned***.
Matthew 12:36-37 KJV

⇒**36** But I tell you, on the day of judgment men will have to give account for ***every idle (inoperative, nonworking)*** word they speak.
37 For by your words you will be justified *and* acquitted, and by your words you will be condemned *and* sentenced.
Matthew 12:36-37 AMPC

On Judgement Day, we will give an account for every idle word we speak. What we say will either justify us to enter Heaven, or condemn us to Hell. In the parable of the ten minas, Jesus says that the nobleman, who has a kingdom, will judge the wicked slave by *his own words*.

⇒21 For I was [constantly] afraid of you, because you are a stern (hard, severe) man; you pick up what you did not lay down, and you reap what you did not sow. 22 He said to the servant, I will judge *and* condemn you out of **your own mouth**, you wicked slave! ***You knew [did you] that I was a stern (hard, severe) man***, picking up what I did not lay down, and reaping what I did not sow?
Luke 19:21-22 AMPC

The Apostle Paul, in both of his letters to Timothy tells the believers to stay away from vain babblings.

⇒20 O Timothy, keep that which is committed to thy trust, **avoiding profane and vain babblings**, and oppositions of science falsely so called:
1 Timothy 6:20 KJV

⇒16 But **shun profane and vain babblings**: for they will **increase unto more ungodliness.**
2 Timothy 2:16 KJV
The word **vain babblings** in the Greek is

kenophōnia- *(empty discussion, discussion of vain and useless matters).*

4

11 If any man speak, <u>**let him speak as the oracles**</u> <u>**of God**</u>**; if any man minister, let him do it as of the ability** which God giveth: **that God in all things may be glorified <u>through Jesus Christ</u>, to whom be praise and dominion for ever and ever. Amen.**
1 Peter 4:11 KJV

⟹The word oracles in the Greek is *logion*- *(the words or utterances of God).*

The Apostle Peter says if ANY man speak let him speak the very words of God. This also includes women. We should desire to speak the Word of God.

29 Let **<u>no</u> foul or polluting language**, nor evil word **<u>nor</u> unwholesome or worthless talk [ever] come out of your mouth**, but only such [speech] as is good and beneficial to the spiritual progress of others, as is fitting to the need and the occasion, that it may be a blessing and give grace (God's favor) to those who hear it.
Ephesians 4:29 AMPC

•**9** With it we bless the Lord and Father, and with it we curse men who were made in God's likeness! **10 Out of the same mouth come forth**

blessing and cursing. <u>These things, my brethren, *ought not to be so*</u>.
James 3:9-10 AMPC

² **To slander *or* abuse *or* speak evil of no one**, to *avoid being contentious*, to be forbearing (yielding, gentle, and conciliatory), and to show <u>unqualified courtesy toward everybody</u>.
Titus 3:2 AMPC

When I played football in high school and college, I used to curse and talk trash. I knew using curse words was wrong, but I thought that God would be okay with it because we played football. In my own understanding, I believed that God was going to forgive me even though I *knowingly* did wrong. <u>I was very foolish</u>. I was foolish because I didn't read the Bible. I lived according to my own assumptions about God instead of reading the Bible.

²⁶ If any man among you seem to be religious, and **bridleth not his tongue**, but *deceiveth* his own heart, this **man's religion is <u>vain</u>**.
James 1:26 KJV

⇒The word **bridleth** in the Greek is *chalinagōgeō- (to* guide, hold in check, restrain).

James, the half-brother of Jesus, said if any man seems to be religious but cannot control his mouth, he is deceived in his heart and his belief is in **vain** or **worthless**. This applies to women as well.

I accepted Jesus as my Lord and Savior my freshman year in high school. I used foul language until my senior year in college. My faith was worthless during that time because I did not control my mouth.

If we read the Bible more, our speech will change, and we will begin to speak the Word of God. We must also train ourselves to **"say less,"** especially when we have nothing good to say.

² **Be not rash with thy mouth**, and <u>let not thine heart be </u>hasty to utter any thing before God: for God is in heaven, and thou upon earth: therefore <u>let **thy words be few**</u>.
Ecclesiastes 5:2 KJV

(STOP CUSSIN')

"If you claim to be religious but don't control your tongue, you are fooling yourself, and your religion is worthless."

James 1:26

• We should ask ourselves as Christians, "Would the words we say daily be allowed in the Kingdom of God?"

• If we have spoken vain and useless words, let us *repent (turn away, don't go back to it)* and the Lord God will forgive us!

CHAPTER 2

SWEAR NOT AT ALL

Thank You Jesus! The Lord is so good! I am truly thankful for the Holy Spirit, who leads us and guides us into all truth.

Let's look at what Jesus says about not swearing oaths.

"Again, ye have heard that it hath been said by them of old time, Thou shalt not forswear thyself, but shalt perform unto the Lord thine oaths: But I say unto you, **Swear not <u>at all</u>**; neither by heaven; for it is God's throne: Nor by the earth; for it is his footstool: neither by Jerusalem; for it is the city of the great King. Neither shalt thou swear by thy head, because thou canst not make one hair white or black. But let your communication be,

Yea, yea; Nay, nay: *for whatsoever is more than these cometh of evil."*
Matthew 5:33-37 KJV

The Greek word for **oath- *horkos*** *(that which has been pledged or promised with an oath).*

⇒Many of the Pharisees *(Matthew 23:16-22)* were allowing people to swear falsely and not keep their oaths. Jesus tells us to not swear oaths at all. People were swearing, knowing they were not going to fulfill their part. Jesus also knows we are not able to control the circumstances around us. If we bind ourselves by an oath and can't fulfill it, we can fall under condemnation.

⇒Jesus made it simple and said, *"Just let your yes be yes, and no be no."* Anything added by swearing oaths would come from evil and not from God.

"But <u>above all things</u>, my brethren, **swear not**, neither by heaven, neither by the earth, **<u>neither by any other oath</u>**: but let your yea be yea; and your nay, nay; ***lest ye*** fall into ***<u>condemnation</u>***."
James 5:12 KJV

In the Old Testament, Numbers 30:2, was the law for swearing oaths or making vows. We see that a **vow** and an **oath** have two separate meanings.

2 If a man **vow a vow** unto the Lord, <u>or</u> **swear an oath** to <u>bind his soul with a bond</u>; he shall not break his word, he shall do according <u>to all</u> that proceedeth out of his mouth.
Numbers 30:2 KJV

- *Hebrew word for **oath**- *shebuw'ah*
- *Hebrew word for **vow**- *nadar*
- Greek Word for **oath**- *horkos* *(that which has been pledged or promised with an oath)*
- Greek word for **vow**- *euchē* *(a prayer to God, a vow, promise to God)*

When someone swears an oath, they are binding themselves to the words that they have sworn to a person. When swearing an oath, people swear by something. They swear by God, other people, or objects. They are invoking someone or something into their promise or agreement.

⇒"For when God made promise to Abraham, because he could **swear by no greater, he**

sware by himself, For men verily swear by the greater: and *an oath for confirmation is to them an end of all strife*. Wherein God, willing more abundantly to shew unto the heirs of promise the immutability of his counsel, **confirmed it by an oath:"**
Hebrews 6:13, 16-17 KJV

Hebrews chapter 6, gives us a good understanding of why people swear oaths. We see that when God made a promise to Abraham, He couldn't swear by anything greater, so He swore by Himself. If an agreement was made and one party didn't uphold their end, an argument would happen. To end the argument the party in violation of the agreement would swear an oath. Oaths were taken to ensure that both parties would uphold their side of the agreement. Agreements or contracts, as we call them today, were confirmed with an oath in the Old Testament. *(Genesis 26:28-31)*

Remember, that Jesus says our own words will either **justify** us or **condemn** us on Judgement Day. I don't think Jesus was kidding when He spoke. *God doesn't say words in vain*. God cannot lie. We must be careful that we are not binding ourselves to agreements with an oath and can't fulfill them completely.

Why do some Christians try to context these Scriptures out of the Bible and say, **"Jesus didn't mean we can't swear oaths at all."**

How do you context these words from the Greek?

Omnyō, mē, holōs (Swear, not, at all) Matthew 5:34

Mēte, tis, allos, horkos (Neither, by any, other, oath) James 5:12

Some people say that Paul swore twice in his letters (*Galatians 1 & 1 Corinthians 4*). Let's say that Paul did swear an oath. Does Paul's actions justify us to disregard what our Lord Jesus commanded? We see in Galatians chapter 2, that Paul had to correct the Apostle Peter publicly because he was not living to the truth of the Gospel (*Galatians*

2:11-14). Paul could have been wrong **if** he did swear in his letters.

We have to remember that these were men, who sometimes missed the leading of the Holy Spirit. The Holy Spirit does not control us. He will lead and guide us. We have a choice to follow His leading or not. **We are called to obey Jesus and His commands.**

Court, Fraternities, & Sororities

What do we do when we go to court?

We have the option to *affirm (to state or assert positively, to confirm, or ratify)* instead of swearing an oath. Some people feel as if affirming is another name for oath. If this is the case, then be led by the Holy Spirit in what He wants you to do and say.

⇒**"You do solemnly state that the testimony you may give in the case now pending before this court shall be the truth, the whole truth,**

and nothing but the truth, under pains and penalties of perjury?"

• We have the legal option to use the statement above in court, instead of swearing an oath.

• When it comes to joining a fraternity or sorority, we should first ask the Lord Jesus if He would want us to be a part of this organization. Does the group agree with the Christian standards of the Bible? Is there anything they are asking me to do that goes against the Bible? If they require that you must swear an oath, I would make the choice <u>to not join</u>. **I would not want to offend my Lord Jesus, by disregarding His commands.**

• **In court, I have sworn an oath in the past. I have repented and asked the Lord to forgive me. I didn't understand the Scriptures back then. I am forgiven and I will not swear an oath at all. If you have sworn an oath, you can do the same and repent. Renounce the oath that you made. God will forgive you!**

MAN'S LAWS CANNOT MAKE MORAL WHAT GOD HAS DECLARED IMMORAL. EVEN IF A SIN IS LEGALIZED, IT'S STILL A SIN IN THE EYES OF GOD.

StandSteadfast

CHAPTER 3

LIVE HOLY & PLAY HOLY

Praise the Lord God for His mercy and grace! During my high school and college years, I would talk trash and sometimes play with malice in my heart. By God's mercy and grace, He convicted me and helped change the way I played the game. During my senior year at Florida State University, I stopped talking trash, fighting, and playing with the intention of hurting people on the field. During that same year, I became a *Sporting News First Team All-American* and *Sports Illustrated Third Team All-American*. I felt like the Lord was rewarding me because I played to glorify Him. I didn't play just for myself. At one point during the season, I was averaging 34.4 yards a return. Praise God! <u>It is possible to play football with the right heart intentions and do well.</u>

¹³ Wherefore **<u>gird up</u>** the loins of your mind, **<u>be sober</u>**, and **hope to the end** for the grace that is to be brought unto you at the revelation of Jesus Christ;
¹⁴ As **<u>obedient</u> children**, not fashioning yourselves according to the former lusts in your ignorance:
¹⁵ But as he which hath called you is holy, **so be ye holy in <u>all manner of conversation</u>**;
1 Peter 1:13-15 KJV

°**Gird up** - *anazōnnymi (to be prepared)*

°**Be Sober** – *nēphō (to be calm, collected in spirit, temperate)*

° **Obedient** – *hypakoē (compliance, submission)*

°**Manner of conversation** – *anastrophē (manner of life, conduct, behavior)*

➤**Anger, wrath, jealousy, bitterness, unforgiveness, selfishness, slander** *(speaking false about someone's character or reputation)***, and malice** *(the desire to harm someone),* **prevent us from being sober minded!**

➤ **These emotions of the flesh cloud our mind and our thinking. It can hinder our focus and hurt our game play. We must live holy and play football holy.**

➤ **Love and respect your teammates and opponents.**

➤ **Forgive when your teammate, coach, or opponent may have done wrong to you. Don't retaliate!**

➤ **Give glory to God when making plays so that your teammates and opponents may be encouraged in the Lord Jesus!**

[26] Let us **not be** desirous of **vainglory, provoking** one another, **envying** one another.
Galatians 5:26 KJV

•**Desirous of vain glory – *kenodoxos*** *(glorying without reason, conceited, eager for empty glory)*

•**Provoking – *prokaleō*** *(to irritate)*

- **Desiring to be selfish to have all the plays and be praised by the fans is** not **pleasing to God.**
- **Compromising your morals** *(lying, taking cheap shots)* **to win a game is** not **pleasing to God.**
- **Being jealous of teammates and opponents is** not **pleasing to God.**
- **Provoking teammates or opponents by talking trash and cussing is** not **pleasing to God.**

Remember, do not worship football, any other sport, person, or thing. We only worship God. I used to worship football, and it was everything to me. Now, I worship God, and Him only I serve. We

can use football as a way to serve the Lord Jesus.
(*Luke 16:15*)

PEOPLE CLAIM
THEY KNOW
GOD,
BUT THEY DENY HIM
BY THE WAY
THEY LIVE.

TITUS 1:16

CHAPTER 4

BE TRUTHFUL IN ALL THINGS

Praise Your holy and mighty name! You are good and good alone Father! Thank You for showing us how to live and speak truthfully in everything we do. When we miss your leading, thank You for being patient with us and guiding us back on the narrow path.

25 Wherefore **putting away lying**, *speak every man __truth__ with his neighbour: for we are members one of another.*
Ephesians 4:25 KJV

⇒Greek word for **lying** is *pseudos-(whatever is not what it seems to be, deceitful, falsehood)*

²⁴ God is a Spirit: and they that worship him **must worship him**
in spirit and in _truth_.
John 4:24 KJV
> ⇒The Greek word for **truth** is _alētheia-(what is_
>
> _true in any matter under consideration, fact)_

⁹ **Lie not one to another**, seeing that ye have put off the old **man with his deeds;**
Colossians 3:9 KJV

⇒4 Neither filthiness, _**nor foolish talking, nor jesting**_, which are not convenient: but rather giving of thanks.
Ephesians 5:3-4 KJV

- The Greek word for **foolish talking** is

  mōrologia-(silly talk, or nonsense)

- The Greek word for **jesting** is _**eutrapelia-**_

  (humour, **facetiousness**-treating serious

  issues with deliberate inappropriate

  humour)

¹⁸ Like a madman who casts firebrands, arrows, and death,¹⁹ So is the man who <u>deceives</u> his

neighbor and then says, **Was I not joking**?
Proverbs 26:18-19 AMPC

· We as believers should be careful to <u>not</u>

<u>prank</u> *(which is practical joke or trick)*, or

joke about one another.

1.Would we like it if God played a joke on us?

2.We should rather encourage one another,

pray for each other, give thanks to the Lord,

have joy and laughter in the Lord.

[2] Then were **our <u>mouths filled with laughter</u>**, and
our tongues <u>with singing</u>. <u>Then they said among</u>
<u>**the nations, The Lord has done great things for**</u>
<u>**them.**</u>
Psalm 126:2 KJV

Our joy and laughter should come from the
Lord. We can also have joy and laughter from our
brothers and sisters in Christ because of fellowship
and the goodness of the Lord.

<u>Pranking or Tricking people.</u>
1. Why do we laugh when someone is deceived
by a prank or trick?

2. Does this come from the Lord?

3. Is this type of behavior pleasing to the Lord?

8 For once you were darkness, but now you are light in the Lord; **walk as children of Light** [lead the lives of those native-born to the Light]. 9 For the fruit (the effect, the product) of the Light *or the Spirit* [consists] in every form of kindly goodness, uprightness of heart, and trueness of life. 10 And <u>try to learn</u> [in your experience] **<u>what is pleasing to the Lord</u>** [let your lives be constant proofs of what is most acceptable to Him]. 11 **Take no part in *and* have no fellowship with the fruitless deeds *and* enterprises of darkness**, but instead [let your lives be so in contrast as to] **<u>expose *and* reprove *and* convict them</u>**.
Ephesians 5:8-11 KJV

IF YOU TRULY
LOVE PEOPLE
TELL THEM
THE
TRUTH

CHAPTER 5

FREEDOM FROM VANITY

Praise God! The more we spend time with the Lord, the more He will lead us to live a life of humility. The closer we get to the Lord; we will have our complete security in Him and not in things of this world.

In 2018, after spending time in prayer and fasting, the Lord had convicted me of vanity (*pride*). I was caught up in my appearance. I was leaving track practice at Cypress Christian School, and I was about to put my earrings back in my ears because we were not allowed to wear them while on campus. The Lord asked me, "**Why do you**

wear them?" I said, "To look a certain way." In my heart, the Lord convicted me of vanity, which is pride. Pride is a sin (*Mark 7:20-23*). It was hard to do, but when I got home, I threw the earrings away in the trash.

As I looked in the Bible, the Lord showed me the meaning behind certain Scriptures. Both apostles, Paul and Peter, say that women should dress modestly, and should not put on jewelry or expensive clothing. Many Christians ignore these Scriptures and say that it is too much. They say we need to change with the culture. The Lord showed me **why both** apostles said not to do that.

When we make ourselves more attractive, it can draw attention, lead to lust in the heart, and our hearts can become prideful in our appearance. They said it to help **prevent *vanity*** and ***lust***.

⇒9 In like manner also, that women adorn themselves in **modest** apparel, with *shamefacedness* and sobriety; **not with broided hair, or gold, or pearls, or costly array;**10 But (which becometh women professing

godliness) with good works.
1 Timothy 2:9-10 KJV

- **Shamefacedness** in the Greek is ***aidōs-**(a sense of shame or honor, modesty, bashfulness, reverence, regard for others)*

3 ***Whose adorning let it not be that outward*** adorning of plaiting the hair, and of wearing of gold, or of putting on of apparel;
4 ***But let it be the hidden man of the heart,*** in that which is not corruptible, even the ornament of a meek and quiet spirit, which is in the sight of God of great price.
5 ***For after this manner in the old time the holy women also, who trusted in God, adorned themselves***, being in subjection unto their own husbands:
1 Peter 3:3-5 KJV

This also applies to men. When the Lord convicted me of being a tempter, it was because I was not dressed modestly. I used to do fitness videos with my shirt off. If a woman would have seen the videos, she could be tempted to lust in her heart after me. I also used to wear tank tops in public. I wore them when it was hot outside but also to be seen. Honestly, I liked the attention. This was wrong of me because my heart motive wasn't pure.

The Lord has also led me to be careful to not wear tight clothing. I can be covered up, but tight clothing can show my muscular shape. Men today have a harder time dealing with lust because many women are wearing tight jeans or skintight yoga pants which shows their shape. We should be mindful of the interest of others before ourselves (*Philippians 2:4*). It is possible to see a person's maturity level by the way they dress. Sometimes, people do not know and need to be told. I was one of those people. Believers should let people know the truth and say, ***"Be careful of what you are wearing because you could be tempting others to sin by the way you dress."***

¹ And [Jesus] said to His disciples, **Temptations (snares, traps set to entice to sin) are sure to come, but woe to him by *or* through whom they come!** ² It would be more profitable for him if a millstone were hung around his neck and he were hurled into the sea than that he should cause to sin *or* be a snare to one of these little ones [lowly in rank or influence].

Luke 17:1-2 AMPC

Some people may say, "I don't want to look weird or old school by dressing modestly." A statement like that may confirm that they are more concerned about how they look (*vanity*) than pleasing the Lord. I usually ask the Lord if what I am wearing is pleasing to Him (*John 8:29*). I want to be more concerned about pleasing the Lord, than how I look to others. If it is hot outside, I will wear a long-sleeved or a short sleeve shirt that is loose. I do this so I am pleasing to the Lord by being modest to unbelievers and my sisters in Christ. It is possible to be modest and look presentable.

⇒16 These six things doth **the Lord hate**: yea, seven are an abomination unto him: 17 **A proud look**, a lying tongue, and hands that shed innocent blood,
Proverbs 6:16-17 KJV
•The Hebrew word *ruwm* for **proud** means-*(to bring up, exalt (self) or magnify oneself)*.

•This can mean someone who is prideful and thinks of themselves more highly than others. *This can also mean someone is prideful in their appearance.*

•There are different levels of pride in oneself. There are different levels of lies. Big lies and little lies. It doesn't matter the level, it is still sin and needs to be repented of.

3 For we [Christians] are the true circumcision, who worship God in spirit *and* by the Spirit of God and exult *and* glory *and* <u>pride ourselves in Jesus Christ</u>, **and <u>put no confidence *or* dependence</u> [on what we are] in the flesh *and* on outward privileges *and* physical advantages *and* external appearances**
Philippians 3:3 AMPC

•God wants us to put our complete trust and confidence in Him.

5 Lean on, trust in, *and* **<u>be confident in the Lord</u> with all your heart *and* mind** and ***do not rely*** on your own insight *or* understanding.
Proverbs 3:5 AMPC

In 2019, while meditating on the Word, the Lord convicted me of dishonesty and falsehood. I am 33 years old and my hairline is starting to recede. I was insecure about it because I felt like it would make me look old. I would put black mascara on my hairline to try and hide my receding hairline. The Lord showed me that I was being dishonest with my image. I was not being truthful in what I really looked like. I began to think, many women put makeup on every day. Are they being truthful in their image?

I decided to do some research about makeup (*cosmetics*) and mascara. There are Scriptures in the Bible that talk about makeup. They use the word face painting (*2 Kings 9:30, Jeremiah 4:30, Ezekiel 23:40,48*). I found out that the word cosmetics comes from the Greek word **Kosmos –** *(the world, of earthly things, order, adornment).* The word **mascara** comes from the Italian language, meaning **mask**. In Arabic, *maskara* means "**buffoon.**" Buffoon means a clown or ridiculous amusing person. Why do many women wear masks every day? It comes from *insecurity*. I was insecure about my hairline, so I tried to mask it or cover it up. This insecurity comes from the world, and not from God. God created us in His image and likeness, why are we concerned with how the world says we should look?

The Lord was not pleased with me putting mascara on my hairline and presenting a false image. <u>I was being vain about my image</u>.

•The Hebrew word for **vain** is *shav'-(emptiness, vanity, falsehood)*. This word is translated in the *King James Version* as, **vain** (22x), **vanity** (22x), **false** (5x), **lying** (2x), **falsely** (1x), and **lies** (1x).

- **Is the Lord pleased with women wearing makeup?**

- **Would the Holy Spirit lead us to be concerned about our outward appearance or the inward, which is the heart?**

[17] Now the Lord is the Spirit, and **where the Spirit of the Lord is**, there is **liberty (*emancipation from bondage, freedom*).**
2 Corinthians 3:17 AMPC

⇒The Holy Spirit wants us to be <u>FREE</u> from vanity!

⇒Choose to be FREE today!

CHAPTER 6

DON'T BE ANXIOUS

Praise the Lord for His mercy and grace. I am truly thankful that the Lord does not put burdens on us that we cannot bear. I am so thankful that we can go to Him in prayer and thanksgiving. I used to get anxious before football games. When I started praying before games and before every play, that anxiety went away.

⁶ Do not fret _or_ have any anxiety about anything, but in every circumstance _and_ in everything, **by prayer and petition** (definite requests), with **thanksgiving**, continue to make your wants known to God. ⁷ And God's peace [shall be yours,

that tranquil state of a soul assured of its salvation through Christ, and so fearing nothing from God and being content with its earthly lot of whatever sort that is, that peace] which transcends all understanding shall garrison *and* **mount guard over your hearts and minds in Christ Jesus.**
Philippians 4:6-7 AMPC

- Paul is telling the believers at Philippi to not be anxious about anything or anyone. This is a *choice* they have to make on their own.

  - He says in everything we should **pray, seek,** and **give thanks** to the Lord. We should make our requests known to the Lord.

  - When we pray, seek, give thanks, and make our requests known to Him, the **PEACE of God** shall keep our hearts and minds through Jesus!

⁷ Casting the whole of your care [all your anxieties, all your worries, all your concerns, once and for all] on Him, for He cares for you affectionately *and* cares about you watchfully.
1 Peter 5:7 AMPC

40 But Martha [**overly occupied and too busy**] **was distracted with much serving**; and she came up to Him and said, Lord, is it nothing to You that my sister has left me to serve alone? Tell her then to help me [to lend a hand and do her part along with me]!

41 But the Lord replied to her by saying, *Martha, Martha, you are anxious and troubled about many things;*

42 **There is need of only one** *or but a few things.* Mary has chosen the good portion [that which is to her advantage], ***which shall not be taken away from her.***
Luke 10:40-42 AMPC

Sometimes we can do too much and it can cause us to be anxious. It is important to ask the Lord what we should get out of our lives, so we are not anxious or worried. How can we not be anxious about sports, jobs, or money? We keep our focus on the Lord. The Lord tells us to not be anxious. We should seek first the Kingdom and His righteousness, and all of our needs will be added unto us.

⇒**25** Therefore I tell you, **stop being perpetually uneasy (anxious and worried)** about your life, what you shall eat *or what you shall drink*; or about your body, what you shall put on. Is not life greater [in quality] than food, and the body [far above and more excellent] than clothing?
Matthew 6:25 AMPC

33 But seek *(aim at and strive after) first of all His kingdom and His righteousness (His way of doing and being right),* and then all these things taken together will be given you besides.
Matthew 6:33 AMPC

CHAPTER 7

THE FORGIVEN MUST FORGIVE

I have done a lot of wrong in my life and I am truly thankful for God's forgiveness towards me. God has truly been merciful to me and has allowed me to live when I should have been dead. I am forever grateful for His mercy and grace.

Lord, I will show that same mercy and grace towards others. I will forgive because You have forgiven me. I will love those who do wrong towards me and pray for those who harm me. Thank You Jesus!

14 For **if ye forgive** men their trespasses, **your heavenly Father will also forgive you**:

¹⁵ But **if ye forgive not** men their trespasses,
neither will your Father forgive your trespasses.
Matthew 6:14-15 KJV

- **We see that God's forgiveness is**
  **conditional****. God will forgive us if we**
  forgive others. If we DO NOT **forgive,**
  then God will not **forgive us of our sins.**
- **We enter into Heaven because we are**
  forgiven. If we are not forgiven, then we
  will NOT **be able to enter into Heaven.**
- **Living in unforgiveness towards others is**
  **choosing** **to not want to go to Heaven.**

³² Then his master called him and said to him, You
contemptible _and_ wicked attendant! I
forgave _and_ **cancelled all that [great] debt of**
yours because you begged me to.

³³ **And should you not have had pity** _and_ **mercy**
on your fellow attendant, as I had
pity _and_ **mercy on you**?

34 And in wrath his master turned him over to the torturers (the jailers), till he should pay all that he owed.

35 So also **My heavenly Father will deal with every one of you if you do not <u>freely forgive</u> your brother <u>from your heart</u> *his offenses*.**
Matthew 18:32-35 AMPC

- **People may hurt you and do wrong to you. Let it go and forgive.**
- **We will reap whatever we sow. If we <u>sow</u> unforgiveness towards others, we will <u>reap</u> unforgiveness from God. (*Galatians 6:7-8*)**
- **God has forgiven us, and we must forgive too!**

Lord, if I'm ever ungrateful, forgive me.

16 Be happy [in your faith] and rejoice and be glad-hearted *continually (always)*;

17 Be unceasing in prayer [praying perseveringly];

18 **Thank [God] in everything** [no matter what the circumstances may be, **be thankful** and give thanks], for this is the will of God for you [who are] in Christ Jesus [the Revealer and Mediator of that will].

1 Thessalonians 5:16-18 AMPC

DAILY REMINDERS

Blessed are the pure in heart; for they shall see God.
-Matthew 5:8

NEVER
WATER YOURSELF DOWN
FOR ANYONE!

SPEAK OF JESUS,
SHARE THE GOSPEL,
TELL YOUR STORY...

WITH BOLDNESS
AND CONFIDENCE,
NEVER LETTING ANYONE
QUENCH THE FIRE IN YOU!

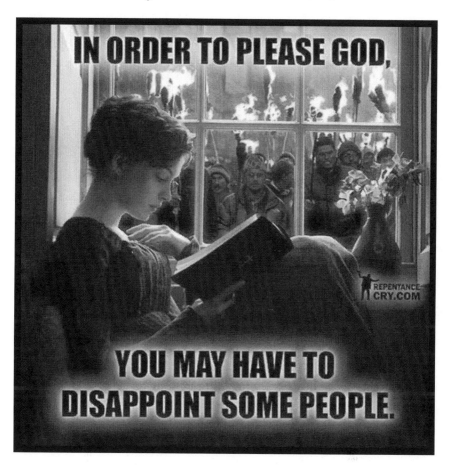

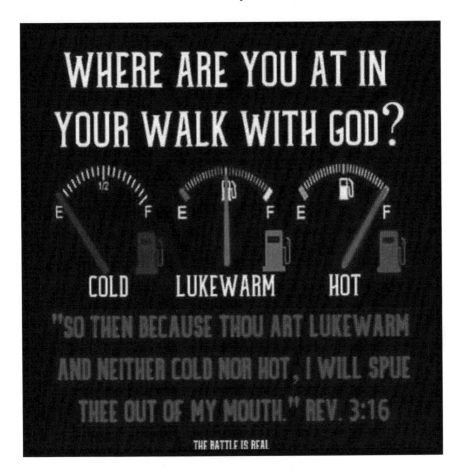

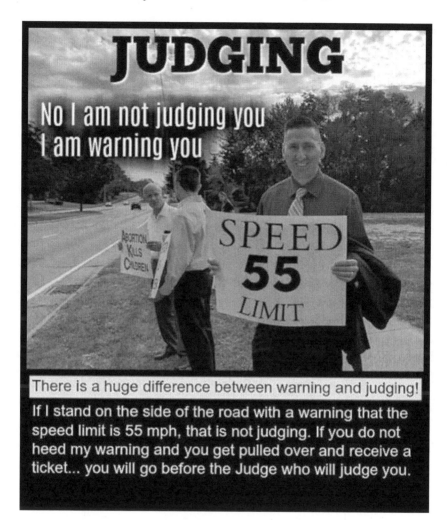

JUDGING

No I am not judging you I am warning you

ABORTION KILLS CHILDREN

SPEED 55 LIMIT

There is a huge difference between warning and judging!

If I stand on the side of the road with a warning that the speed limit is 55 mph, that is not judging. If you do not heed my warning and you get pulled over and receive a ticket... you will go before the Judge who will judge you.

A DISCIPLE OF CHRIST HAS A GROWING DRIVE TO OBEY REGARDLESS OF THE CONSEQUENCES, SACRIFICE, OR COST.

The most important thing we have to do in this world is to PREPARE OURSELVES FOR ETERNITY

In order to
FOLLOW
Jesus,
You will have to
UNFOLLOW
The world.

Made in the USA
Lexington, KY
15 December 2019